Diabetic Meal Prep Cookbook

*Flavorful and Heart-Healthy Low-Carb Dishes
to Manage or Avoid Diabetes*

Brittany Kale

work can be in any fashion deemed liable for any hardship or damages that may befall them after undertaking information described herein.

Additionally, the information in the following pages is intended only for informational purposes and should thus be thought of as universal. As befitting its nature, it is presented without assurance regarding its prolonged validity or interim quality. Trademarks that are mentioned are done without written consent and can in no way be considered an endorsement from the trademark holder.

TABLE OF CONTENTS

INTRODUCTION

Diabetes is a disease that affects a lot of people.

Diabetes has to constantly watch what they eat, and that can get very tedious. They have to be very careful with the number of carbohydrates they eat as well. To control diabetes and its many side effects, diabetes has to make sure to have a healthy diet plan that is easy to follow.

If you have diabetes, insulin resistance diets can go a long way to help manage your health conditions so you can live healthier. Following the insulin resistance diet plan doesn't mean you need special foods. All you need to lower your risk of diabetes is to eat more fruits, fish, vegetables, and whole grains, and to eat less red meats, unhealthy fat, processed starch, and sugar. But sometimes, it's challenging to change diet and lifestyle.

By simply checking your blood sugar levels and adjusting where you can, you'll soon see that diabetes doesn't have to be the big problem you originally thought it to be.

But sometimes, it's challenging to change diet and lifestyle.

In this book, you will find recommended meals for diabetes, but of course also delicious recipes for the whole family.

Just, make sure you pay attention to the quality of the ingredients and prefer organic food. This is not just good for the environment but also for your body.

Have fun, good luck, and Bon appetite!

DIABETIC BREAKFAST

CRANBERRY ORANGE MACADAMIA SCONES

Time required:
35 minutes

Servings: 08

INGREDIENTS

2 cups roasted, unsalted macadamia nut

1 cup chopped fresh cranberries

2 eggs

1/3 cup sifted coconut flour

1/3 cup orange juice

¼ cup pure maple syrup

¼ cup melted coconut oil

1 tsp baking soda

1 tsp pure vanilla extract

¼ tsp sea salt

Zest from 1 orange

STEPS FOR COOKING

1. Preheat oven to 350F. Grind nuts in a blender, until coarse meal forms.

2. Add them to a mixing bowl, also add flour, soda, and salt, and stir to combine.

3. Add eggs, syrup, vanilla extract, and juice and blend with a hand mixer until smooth. Continue mixing, slowly pour in coconut oil. Set aside for 5 minutes.

4. Add cranberries and zest.

5. Spoon the mixture on a baking sheet covered with parchment. Make 8 balls and flatten them slightly. Bake for 20-25 minutes.

6. Serve cooled.

BACON, SPINACH, AND MUSHROOM CASSEROLE

Time required:
30 minutes

Servings: 04

INGREDIENTS

2 ½ lbs good quality smoked bacon

3 big handfuls of fresh spinach

1 lb button mushrooms

1 large onion

2 garlic cloves

2 tbsp butter

salt and pepper to taste

STEPS FOR COOKING

1. Cut the bacon into medium-sized pieces.
2. Slice the mushrooms.
3. Chop the onion.
4. Mince the garlic.
5. Heat a large casserole over medium flame and cook bacon, checking it's still soft.
6. Add the onion and garlic, then cook for 5 mins, until soft.
7. Add the mushrooms, then cook for 8 mins.
8. Add the spinach and butter, cover, and cook for another 4 mins, until the spinach is well cooked.
9. Add some salt and pepper to taste.

YOGURT AND KALE SMOOTHIE

Time required:
10 minutes

Servings: 01

INGREDIENTS	STEPS FOR COOKING

Cup whole milk yogurt

Cup baby kale greens

1 pack stevia

1 tablespoon MCT oil

Tablespoon sunflower seeds cup of water

1. Add listed ingredients to the blender.
2. Blend until you get a smooth and creamy texture.
3. Serve chilled and enjoy!

WHOLE-GRAIN DUTCH BABY PANCAKE

Time required:
30 minutes

Servings: 04

INGREDIENTS

2 tablespoons coconut oil

1/2 cup whole-wheat flour

¼ cup skim milk

3 large eggs

1 teaspoon vanilla extract

1/2 teaspoon baking powder

¼ teaspoon salt

¼ teaspoon ground cinnamon

Powdered sugar, for dusting

STEPS FOR COOKING

1. Preheat the oven to 400F.

2. Put the coconut oil in a medium oven-safe skillet, and place the skillet in the oven to melt the oil while it preheats.

3. In a blender, combine the flour, milk, eggs, vanilla, baking powder, salt, and cinnamon. Process until smooth.

4. Carefully remove the skillet from the oven and tilt to spread the oil around evenly.

5. Pour the batter into the skillet and return it to the oven for 23 to 25 minutes, until the pancake puffs and lightly browns.

6. Remove, dust lightly with powdered sugar, cut into 4 wedges, and serve.

CANTALOUPE SMOOTHIE

Time required:
11 minutes

Servings: 02

INGREDIENTS

¾ cup carrot juice

4 cups cantaloupe,
sliced into cubes

Pinch of salt

Frozen melon balls

Fresh basil

STEPS FOR COOKING

1. Add the carrot juice and cantaloupe cubes to a blender. Sprinkle with salt.
2. Process until smooth.
3. Transfer to a bowl.
4. Chill in the refrigerator for at least 30 minutes.
5. Top with the frozen melon balls and basil before serving.

CHEESE AND EGG BREAKFAST SANDWICH

Time required:
16 minutes

Servings: 01

INGREDIENTS

1-2 eggs
1-2 slices of cheddar
or Swiss cheese
A bit of butter
1 roll sliced in half
(Kaiser Bun, or
English muffin, etc.)

STEPS FOR COOKING

1. Butter your sliced roll on both sides. Place the eggs in an oven-safe dish and whisk. Add seasoning if you wish such as dill, chives, oregano, and salt. Place the egg dish, roll, and cheese into the air fryer.

2. Make assured the buttered sides of the roll are in front of upwards. Set the air fryer to 390 Fahrenheit with a Cooking Time of 6- minutes. Remove the ingredients when Cooking Time is completed by air fryer.

3. Place the egg and cheese between the pieces of roll and serve warm. You might like to try adding slices of avocado and tomatoes to this breakfast sandwich!

ZUCCHINI AND BLUEBERRY BREAD

Time required:
25 minutes

Servings: 06

INGREDIENTS

For the bread:
Butter (softened)
½ cup erythritol
¾ cup
3 large eggs
1 tablespoon lemon juice
1 tablespoon lemon zest
1 teaspoon vanilla extract
2 cups almond flour (blanched)
2 teaspoons baking powder (gluten-free)
¼ teaspoon sea salt
1 ½ cups zucchini (grated)
1 cup blueberries
For the lemon glaze:

STEPS FOR COOKING

1. Start by preheating the oven by setting the temperature to 325 degrees Fahrenheit.

2. Take a loaf pan measuring 9x5 inches and line it with parchment paper. Set aside.

3. Take a large glass bowl and toss in the erythritol and butter; use a whisk to beat them together until the mixture is fluffy.

4. Add in the eggs, lemon zest, vanilla extract, and lemon juice; continue beating until all ingredients are well incorporated.

5. Add in the almond flour, sea salt, and baking powder; mix well.

6. Place the grated zucchini into a muslin cloth or a cheesecloth and squeeze out as much liquid as you can.

7. Once almost all of the moisture has been released, transfer the zucchini

¼ cup erythritol (powdered)

4 teaspoons lemon juice

into the almond flour mixture. Use a spatula to fold it into the mixture until all ingredients are nicely combined.

8. Toss the blueberries into the zucchini and flour mixture and gently fold until well incorporated.

9. Pour the prepared batter into the loaf pan lined with parchment paper. Use the back of a spoon to even the top of the batter.

10. Place the loaf pan into the preheated oven and bake for about 70 minutes. Insert a toothpick to ensure the bread is properly cooked.

11. Remove the loaf pan from the oven and set it aside until it cools down completely.

12. While the bread is cooling down, prepare the glaze by adding erythritol and lemon juice to a mixing bowl. Whisk until both ingredients are nicely combined and smooth in texture.

13. Transfer the zucchini and blueberry bread onto a serving platter and drizzle with the prepared lemon glaze.

14. Serve!

STRAWBERRY COCONUT BAKE

Time required:
52 minutes

Servings: 04

INGREDIENTS	STEPS FOR COOKING

INGREDIENTS

½ cup chopped walnuts

2 cups unsweetened coconut flakes

1 tsp. cinnamon

¼ cup chia seeds

2 cups diced strawberries

1 ripe banana mashed

1 tsp. baking soda

4 large eggs

¼ tsp. salt

1 cup unsweetened nut milk

2 tbsp. coconut oil, melted

STEPS FOR COOKING

1. Preheat your oven to 375°F. Grease a square 8-inch pan and set it aside.

2. Combine the dried ingredients in a big bowl: walnuts, chia seeds, cinnamon, salt, and baking soda.

3. Whisk the eggs and milk together in a smaller dish. Now, add mashed banana and coconut oil to the mixture. To dry, add the wet ingredients and blend properly. Fold the strawberries in.

4. Bake for about 40 minutes, or until the top is golden and solid.

5. And serve hot!

DEXOT APPLE SMOOTHIE

Time required:
5 minutes

Servings: 02

INGREDIENTS

2 cups spring water

2 cups amaranth greens

2 medium fresh apples, cored

1 key lime, juiced

¼ avocado

STEPS FOR COOKING

1. With a high-powered blender, combine all the ingredients.
2. Cover then process at high speed for 1 minute.

ALMOND WAFFLES WITH BERRIES

Time required:
25 minutes

Servings: 04

INGREDIENTS

2 eggs

250 g ground almonds

3 tbsp coconut flakes

1 tbsp coconut milk

1 teaspoon of tartar baking powder

1 pinch of vanilla flavor

1 pinch of cinnamon

150 g blackberries

STEPS FOR COOKING

1. Beat the eggs in a bowl and whisk. Add the almonds, then stir until smooth.

2. Now add coconut flakes, coconut milk, baking powder, vanilla, and cinnamon, and stir well.

3. Heat up waffle iron, add 1 large spoonful of batter and fry the waffles.

4. In the meantime, finely puree the blackberries with the hand blender.

5. Serve the waffles with the berry puree.

QUINOA BERRY PORRIDGE

Time required:
35 minutes

Servings: 01

INGREDIENTS

100 g quinoa

300 ml almond drink - unsweetened

½ stick of cinnamon

¼ teaspoon ground vanilla

1 teaspoon turmeric powder

150 g berries - mixed

2 tbsp pumpkin seeds

2 tbsp almonds

STEPS FOR COOKING

1. Rinse the quinoa thoroughly with water. Then briefly bring to the boil with the almond drink, cinnamon, vanilla, and turmeric in a saucepan and simmer over low heat for 15 minutes. Remove the pot from the stove and let everything swell for another 10-12 minutes. Take the cinnamon stick out of the pot.

2. Wash and dry the berries. Chop the pumpkin seeds and almonds and roast them lightly in a pan if necessary.

3. Spread the quinoa porridge on bowls and sprinkle the berries, pumpkin seeds, and almonds on top.

OATMEAL - BROWN MILLET MUESLI

Time required:
5 minutes

Servings: 01

INGREDIENTS	STEPS FOR COOKING

200g natural yogurt

1 teaspoon natural honey

2 teaspoons of ground brown millet

20g oatmeal

2 apples or 2 servings of the fruit of your choice

10g coconut flakes

1. Cut the fruit open and prepare everything into muesli in a bowl.
2. Sweeten with a little honey and you're done.

SALTY MACADAMIA CHOCOLATE SMOOTHIE

Time required:
5 minutes

Servings: 01

INGREDIENTS

STEPS FOR COOKING

2 tablespoons macadamia nuts, salted

1/3 cup chocolate whey protein powder, low carb

1 cup almond milk, unsweetened

1. Add the listed ingredients to your blender and blend until you have a smooth mixture

2. Chill and enjoy it!

BACON AND CHICKEN GARLIC WRAP

Time required:
25 minutes

Servings: 04

INGREDIENTS

*chicken fillet, cut
into small cubes*

*8-9 thin slices bacon,
cut to fit cubes*

*6 garlic cloves,
minced*

STEPS FOR COOKING

1. Preheat your oven to 400 degrees F
2. Line a baking tray with aluminum foil
3. Add minced garlic to a bowl and rub each chicken piece with it
4. Wrap bacon piece around each garlic chicken bite
5. Secure with toothpick
6. Transfer bites to the baking sheet, keeping a little bit of space between them
7. Bake for about 15-20 minutes until crispy
8. Serve and enjoy!

SHIITAKE MEAT LOAF

Time required:
90 minutes

Servings: 04

INGREDIENTS

1½ lbs ground grass-fed beef

¼ cup sliced shiitake mushrooms

2 plum tomatoes, chopped

1 omega

3 egg

1 tbsp extra virgin olive oil

1 tbsp freshly ground flaxseed

½ tsp onion powder

½ tsp garlic powder

¼ cup red wine

STEPS FOR COOKING

1. Preheat oven to 350F.
2. Heat oil in a pan, add mushrooms, and fry for 5 minutes over medium heat.
3. Add tomatoes and cook for 5 minutes. Remove from the pan, cool for 5 minutes, and put in a blender.
4. Combine mixture with meat, spices, egg, and flaxseed in a bowl, mix thoroughly, and put in a loaf pan. Drizzle with red wine.
5. Bake meatloaf for 75 minutes. Cool for 5 minutes before serving.

CLASSIC EGG SALAD

Time required:
20 minutes

Servings: 04

INGREDIENTS

6 large eggs

3 tbsp mayonnaise

2 celery stalks

½ bunch chives, chopped

a squeeze of lemon juice

salt and pepper to taste

STEPS FOR COOKING

1. Chop the stalks and chives.

2. Pour cold water in a pot, put eggs in it and bring to a boil, then cover turn off the heat and leave for 7 minutes.

3. Rinse the eggs with cold water for 1-2 minutes.

4. Peel the eggs and put them in a bowl with the mayonnaise and mash together with a fork.

5. Add salt, pepper, celery, chives, and lemon juice.

PEANUT BUTTER & BANANA BREAKFAST SANDWICH

Time required:
7 minutes

Servings: 01

INGREDIENTS

STEPS FOR COOKING

2 slices of whole wheat bread

1 teaspoon of sugar-free maple syrup

1 sliced banana

2 tablespoons of peanut butter

1. Evenly coat both sides of the slices of bread with peanut butter. Add the sliced banana and drizzle with some sugar-free maple syrup. Heat in the air fryer to 330°Fahrenheit for 6 minutes. Serve warm.

BREAKFAST FRITTATA

Time required:
15 minutes

Servings: 03

INGREDIENTS

6 eggs

8 cherry tomatoes, halved

2 tablespoons parmesan cheese, shredded

1 Italian sausage, diced

Salt and pepper to taste

STEPS FOR COOKING

1. Preheat your air fryer to 355°Fahrenheit. Add the tomatoes and sausage to the baking dish. Place the baking dish into an air fryer and cook for 5-minutes.

2. Meanwhile, add eggs, salt, pepper, cheese, and oil into the mixing bowl and whisk well. Remove the baking dish from the air fryer and pour the egg mixture on top, spreading evenly. Placing the dish back into the air fryer and bake for an additional 5-minutes.

3. Remove from air fryer and slice into wedges and serve.

MORNING MINI CHEESEBURGER SLIDERS

Time required:
16 minutes

Servings: 06

INGREDIENTS

1 lb. ground beef

6 slices of cheddar cheese

6 dinner rolls

Salt and black pepper to taste

STEPS FOR COOKING

1. Preheat your air fryer to 390°Fahrenheit. Form 6 beef patties each about 2.5 ounces and season with salt and black pepper. Add the burger patties to the cooking basket and cook them for 10-minutes.

2. Remove the burger patties from the air fryer; place the cheese on top of the burgers and return to the air fryer and cook for another minute.

3. Remove and put burgers on dinner rolls and serve warm.

EGG AND AVOCADO BREAKFAST BURRITO

Time required:
15 minutes

Servings: 04

INGREDIENTS

2 hard-boiled egg whites, chopped

1 hard-boiled egg, chopped

1 avocado, peeled, pitted, and chopped

1 red bell pepper, chopped

3 tablespoons low-sodium salsa (optional)

1 slice low-sodium, low-fat American cheese, torn into pieces

4 low-sodium whole-wheat flour tortillas

STEPS FOR COOKING

1. In a medium bowl, thoroughly mix the egg whites, egg, avocado, red bell pepper, salsa, and cheese.

2. Place the tortillas on a work surface and evenly divide the filling among them. Fold in the edges and roll-up. Secure the burritos with toothpicks if necessary.

3. Put the burritos in the air fryer basket. Air fry at 390ºF (199ºC) for 3 to 5 minutes, or until the burritos are light golden brown and crisp. Serve with more salsa (if using).

DIABETIC LUNCH

CHILLED CUCUMBER AND LIME SOUP

Time required:
25 minutes

Servings: 02

INGREDIENTS

1 cucumber, peeled

½ zucchini, peeled

1 tbsp. freshly squeezed lime juice

1 tbsp. fresh cilantro leaves

1 garlic clove, crushed

¼ tsp. sea salt

STEPS FOR COOKING

1. In a blender, blend together the cucumber, zucchini, lime juice, cilantro, garlic, and salt until well combined, then add more salt, if necessary.

2. Pour into a large bowl and enjoy immediately, or refrigerate for about 20 minutes to chill before serving.

LEMON CAULIFLOWER AND PINE NUTS

Time required:
25 minutes

Servings: 04

INGREDIENTS	STEPS FOR COOKING
1 tsp. lemon zest	1. Preheat your oven to 400°F.
¼ tsp. sea salt	2. In a large bowl, combine the ingredients, then set onto a baking sheet.
1 package cauliflower florets	3. Bake for 20 minutes, serve and enjoy!
2 tbsp. extra virgin olive oil	
2 tbsp. pine nuts	
1 tbsp. parsley, fresh flat-leaf	
1 ½ tsp. lemon juice	
¼ tsp. fresh ground black pepper	

CHICKEN THIGHS

Time required:
50 minutes

Servings: 04

INGREDIENTS

4 bone-in skinless chicken thighs
½ tsp. ginger
1 tbsp. olive oil
2 tbsp. soy sauce
¼ tsp. dry mustard
1 garlic clove
¼ tsp. red pepper
¼ tsp. all-spice

STEPS FOR COOKING

1. Preheat the oven to 400°F and sauté the minced garlic, ground allspice, ground ginger, crushed red pepper, and mustard in hot oil for 5 minutes. Remove from heat.

2. Whisk in soy sauce, then place the chicken thighs on a baking sheet. Add the garlic mixture over the chicken, and toss.

ASPARAGUS AND CHICKEN SALAD

Time required:
30 minutes

Servings: 04

INGREDIENTS

500 g asparagus

Sea salt, pepper from the mill

1 ripe mango

1 small Roman salad

400 g chicken breast fillet

6 tbsp rapeseed oil

1 red onion

4 tbsp raspberry vinegar

2 tbsp mixed herbs

100 g whole grain baguette

STEPS FOR COOKING

1. Peel the asparagus and cut it into pieces. Then cook in boiling salted water for about 5-10 minutes. Peel the mango and cut the flesh into narrow strips. Divide the lettuce and pluck it into bite-sized pieces.

2. Wash and slice the meat. Then salt, pepper, and fry in a pan with 2 tablespoons of oil all around for about 5 minutes. Take it out and set it aside.

3. Peel the onion, then cut it into fine rings. Then sauté in the frying fat until translucent. Deglaze with the vinegar and stir in the remaining oil. Season the dressing and refine it with herbs.

4. Mix all salad ingredients with the dressing and serve with the baguette.

LIVER DUMPLING SOUP

Time required:
50 minutes

Servings: 04

INGREDIENTS

150 g beef liver

1 onion

½ bunch of parsley

1 tbsp rapeseed oil

70 g breadcrumbs

1 egg

Sea salt, pepper, nutmeg

2 carrots

100 g celery

4 spring onions

1 tbsp olive oil

1 bay leaf

1 l vegetable stock

STEPS FOR COOKING

1. Grind the liver in the food processor. Peel the onion and finely chop it with parsley. Heat the oil in a saucepan and sauté the parsley and onions.

2. Knead the liver with breadcrumbs, parsley and onion mixture, and the egg, then season. Shape the mixture into 12 dumplings and place in the refrigerator.

3. Now wash the vegetables, slice the carrots, cut the celery, and spring onions into fine rings.

4. Heat the olive oil in a saucepan and sauté the vegetables with the bay leaf for about 4-5 minutes. Pour in the broth and cook the soup over medium heat for about 10 minutes.

5. Add the dumplings to the soup and cook for about 10 minutes. When the dumplings rise to the surface, the soup is ready to serve.

FISH STEW

Time required:
50 minutes

Servings: 04

INGREDIENTS

4 tomatoes

200 ml of cream

300 ml of broth

4 cl vermouth

200 g frozen peas

2 tbsp light sauce
thickener

2 teaspoons of
lemon juice

Sea salt, pepper

200 g whole wheat
pasta

2 tbsp pasture
butter

200 g sugar snap
peas

500 g haddock loin

2 teaspoons of dill

STEPS FOR COOKING

1. Cut the tomatoes crosswise at the top
   and pour hot water over them, then
   peel, halve and dice finely.

2. Bring the cream with the broth and
   wormwood to the boil briefly, then
   add the peas and cook for about 5-6

3. minutes. Scatter the sauce thickener,
   bring to the boil again and season
   with lemon juice, pepper, and salt.

4. Meanwhile, cook the pasta in another
   pot for 8-10 minutes.

5. In a pan, sauté the tomatoes in hot
   butter for about 1-2 minutes, then stir
   in the pasta and season to taste.

6. Lightly salt the fish, then cut it bite-
   sized and add to the sauce with the
   snow peas and let it simmer for about
   6-10 minutes.

7. Arrange the ragout with the pasta and
   serve.

PASTA SALAD

Time required:
30 minutes

Servings: 04

INGREDIENTS

STEPS FOR COOKING

8 oz. whole-wheat pasta

2 tomatoes

(5-oz) pkg spring mix

9 slices bacon

1/3 cup mayonnaise (reduced-fat)

1 tbsp. Dijon mustard

3 tbsp. apple cider vinegar

1/4 tsp. salt

1/2 tsp. pepper

1. Cook pasta.
2. Chilled pasta, chopped tomatoes, and spring mix in a bowl.
3. Crumble cooked bacon over pasta.
4. Combine mayonnaise, mustard, vinegar, salt, and pepper in a small bowl.
5. Pour dressing over pasta, stirring to coat.

CREAMY TACO SOUP

Time required:
30 minutes

Servings: 02

INGREDIENTS	STEPS FOR COOKING

INGREDIENTS

3/4 lb. ground sirloin

1/2 (8-oz) cream cheese

1/2 onion

clove garlic

1 (10-oz) can tomatoes and green chiles

1 (14.5-oz) can beef broth

1/4 cup heavy cream

1,5 tsp. cumin

1/2 tsp. chili powder

STEPS FOR COOKING

1. Cook beef, chopped onion, and minced garlic until the meat is browned and crumbly; drain and return to pot.

2. Add ground cumin, chili powder, and cream cheese cut into small pieces and softened, stirring until cheese is melted.

3. Add diced tomatoes, broth, and cream; bring to a boil, and simmer for 10 Minutes. Season with pepper and salt to taste.

WRAPPED SALMON

Time required:
30 minutes

Servings: 04

INGREDIENTS

6 cabbage leaves, sliced in half

4 medium salmon steaks, skinless

2 red bell peppers, chopped

Some coconut oil

1 yellow onion, chopped

A pinch of sea salt

Black pepper to taste

STEPS FOR COOKING

1. Put water in a large saucepan, bring to a boil over medium-high heat, add cabbage leaves, blanch them for 2 minutes, transfer to a bowl filled with cold water, and pat dry.

2. Season salmon steaks with a pinch of sea salt and black pepper to taste and wrap each in 3 cabbage leaf halves.

3. Heat up a pan with some coconut oil over medium-high heat, add onion and bell pepper, stir and cook for 4 minutes.

4. Add wrapped salmon, place pan in the oven at 350 degrees F, and bake for 12 minutes.

5. Divide salmon and veggies between plates and serve.

6. Enjoy!

SHRIMP WITH MANGO AND AVOCADO MIX

Time required:
15 minutes

Servings: 02

INGREDIENTS

1 avocado, pitted, peeled, and chopped

1 pound shrimp, peeled and deveined

1 tomato, chopped

1 mango, peeled and chopped

1 jalapeno, chopped

1 tablespoon lime juice

A drizzle of olive oil

¼ cup green onions, chopped

4 garlic cloves, minced

A pinch of sea salt

Black pepper to taste

STEPS FOR COOKING

1. In a bowl, mix lime juice with jalapeno, mango, tomato, avocado, and green onions, stir well and leave aside.

2. Heat up a pan with the oil over medium-high heat, add garlic, stir and cook for 2 minutes.

3. Add shrimp, a pinch of sea salt, and black pepper, stir and cook for 5 minutes.

4. Divide shrimp between plates, add mango and avocado mix on the side, and serve.

5. Enjoy!

PESTO CHICKEN

Time required:
40 minutes

Servings: 02

INGREDIENTS

1 cup fresh basil

3 tablespoons olive oil

1 tablespoon walnuts, chopped

1 oz Parmesan, grated

9 oz chicken breast, skinless, boneless

¼ teaspoon ground coriander

STEPS FOR COOKING

1. Make the pesto sauce: blend together fresh basil, olive oil, and walnuts.

2. When the mixture is smooth, add grated Parmesan and pulse it for 5 seconds more.

3. Rub the chicken breast with ground coriander and place it in the baking dish.

4. Pour the pesto sauce over the chicken and flatten it gently with the help of the spatula.

5. Cover the chicken with foil and secure the edges.

6. Transfer the baking dish in the preheated to 375F oven and cook for 30 minutes.

CHEESY CHICKPEA AND COURGETTE BURGERS

Time required:
25 minutes

Servings: 02

INGREDIENTS

1 can chickpeas, drained

3 tablespoons coriander

1-ounce cheddar cheese, shredded

2 eggs, beaten

1 teaspoon garlic puree

1 zucchini, spiralized

1 red onion, diced

1 teaspoon chili powder

1 teaspoon mixed spice

Salt and pepper to taste

1 teaspoon cumin

STEPS FOR COOKING

1. Mix your ingredients in a mixing bowl.
2. Shape portions of the mixture into burgers.
3. Place in the air fryer at 300°Fahrenheit for 15-minutes.

CRANBERRY PORK LOIN

Time required:
25 minutes

Servings: 02

INGREDIENTS

1 tbsp. cooking oil

1 tbsp. honey

1/8 tsp. salt

1/8 tsp. ground nutmeg

1/8 tsp. ground black pepper

2 tbsp. frozen orange juice concentrate, thawed

¼ tsp. ground ginger

½ cup] whole cranberry sauce

4 (5 ounces) boneless pork loin chops, cut ½-inch thick

STEPS FOR COOKING

1. Coat a skillet with nonstick cooking spray and place over medium-high heat. Sprinkle salt and pepper on both sides of the chops and put it on the skillet. Reduce the heat to medium and let the chops cook until done.

2. Make sure you turn the chops, then remove the chops from the skillet and cover with foil. Add orange juice concentrate, honey, nutmeg, ginger, and cranberry sauce in a bowl and mix. Add the mixture to the skillet and cook for 2 minutes until the sauce thickens. Pour over the chops and serve.

BALSAMIC AND DIJON CHICKEN

Time required:
17 minutes

Servings: 02

INGREDIENTS	STEPS FOR COOKING

INGREDIENTS

3 tbsp. balsamic vinegar

2 tsp. snipped fresh thyme

1/3 cup Dijon-style mustard

2 cloves garlic, minced

4 pcs skinless, boneless chicken breast halves

Fresh thyme sprigs

STEPS FOR COOKING

1. In a resealable plastic bag placed over a shallow dish, add the chicken and set aside. Prepare the marinade by stirring the balsamic vinegar, mustard, thyme, and garlic until smooth.

2. Pour the marinade on the chicken inside the plastic and seal the bag. Turn bag to coat the chicken and leave in the fridge for 24 hours. Turn the bag if needed.

3. Drain the chicken, don't discard the marinade. Place the chicken on the grill directly over coals. Grill, the chicken for 7 minutes and brush with marinade. Turn the chicken and coat again with marinade. Garnish with thyme sprigs. Serve.

RED CLAM SAUCE AND PASTA

Time required:
4 hours

Servings: 04

INGREDIENTS	STEPS FOR COOKING

1 onion, diced

¼ cup fresh parsley, diced

2 6 ½ oz. cans clams, chopped, undrained

14 ½ oz. tomatoes, diced, undrained

6 oz. tomato paste

2 cloves garlic, diced

1 bay leaf

1 tbsp. sunflower oil

1 tsp. Splenda

1 tsp. basil

½ tsp. thyme

½ Homemade Pasta, cook & drain

1. Heat oil in a small skillet over med-high heat, then add onion and cook until tender, add garlic and cook 1 minute more. Transfer to crockpot.

2. Add remaining ingredients, except pasta, cover, and cook on low for 3-4 hours.

3. Discard bay leaf and serve over cooked pasta.

CORN TORTILLAS AND SPINACH SALAD

Time required:
8 minutes

Servings: 04

INGREDIENTS

2 cups baby spinach, chopped

4 corn tortillas

2 tbsp. red onion, chopped

4 cherry tomatoes, whole

2 tsp. balsamic vinegar

8 olives, ripe and pitted

1 tbsp. extra-virgin olive oil

Salt and pepper to taste

STEPS FOR COOKING

1. Heat your tortillas according to their package instructions.

2. Mix the remaining ingredients in a bowl.

3. Serve the tortillas along with your salad and enjoy!

CHICKEN CORDON BLEU

Time required:
43 minutes

Servings: 08

INGREDIENTS

8 chicken breasts,
boneless and
skinless

½ cup fat-free sour
cream

2/3 cup skim milk

1 ½ cups mozzarella
cheese, grated

8 slices ham

1 cup corn flakes,
crushed

1 can (low-fat)
condensed cream of
chicken soup

1 tsp. lemon juice

1 tsp. paprika

½ tsp. garlic powder

½ tsp. black pepper

¼ tsp. sea salt

STEPS FOR COOKING

1. Heat your oven to 350°F, then spray a
   baking dish lightly with cooking spray.

2. Flatten the chicken breasts to ¼-inch
   thick.

3. Sprinkle with pepper and top with a
   slice of ham and 3 tbsp. cheese down
   the middle.

4. Roll up, and tuck ends under and
   secure with toothpicks.

5. Pour the milk into a shallow bowl. In
   another bowl, combine corn flakes
   and seasoning.

6. Dip the chicken into milk, roll in the
   cornflake mixture, and then place on a
   prepared baking dish.

7. Bake until your chicken is cooked
   through.

8. In a small pan, whisk the soup, lemon
   juice, and sour cream until well

Nonstick cooking spray as needed

combined. Cook over medium heat until hot.

9. Remove the toothpicks from your chicken and place them onto serving plates.

10. Top with sauce, serve and enjoy!

MEATBALLS

Time required:
35 minutes

Servings: 04

INGREDIENTS

500 g minced meat

2 red onions

1 clove of garlic

1 cm of fresh ginger

1 organic egg

1 tbsp soy sauce

2 tbsp chopped coriander

Sea salt, pepper

250 g lamb's lettuce

1 radicchio

1 tbsp raspberry jelly

2 tbsp raspberry vinegar

5 tbsp walnut oil

1 teaspoon mustard

3 tbsp rapeseed oil

3 tbsp chopped peanuts

STEPS FOR COOKING

1. Peel an onion and chop it very finely. Mash the garlic. Peel and finely chop the ginger. Then mix everything with the minced meat, egg, soy sauce, 3 tablespoons of water, coriander, salt, and pepper and cover and let stand for about 15 minutes.

2. Clean the salads and pluck them bite-sized. Peel the other onion and cut it into fine rings.

3. Mix the jelly with vinegar, walnut oil, and mustard and season with salt and pepper.

4. Shape the minced meat mixture into small meatballs and fry on both sides in a pan with oil.

5. Mix the salads with the onion rings and serve with the meatballs. Sprinkle the salad with peanuts, drizzle with the dressing and serve everything.

HAM AND EGG CUPS

Time required:
25 minutes

Servings: 04

INGREDIENTS

STEPS FOR COOKING

5 slices ham

4 tbsp. cheese

1,5 tbsp. cream

3 egg whites

1,5 tbsp. pepper
(green)

tsp. salt

pepper to taste

1. Preheat oven to 350 F.
2. Arrange each slice of thinly sliced ham into 4 muffin tin.
3. Put 1/4 of grated cheese into a ham cup.
4. Mix eggs, cream, salt, and pepper, then divide it into 2 tins.
5. Bake in oven 15 Minutes; after baking, sprinkle with green onions.

CAPRESE TURKEY BURGERS

Time required:
20 minutes

Servings: 04

INGREDIENTS

1/2 lb. 93% lean ground turkey

2 (1,5-oz) whole wheat hamburger buns (toasted)

1/4 cup shredded mozzarella cheese (part-skim)

egg

1 big tomato

1 small clove garlic

4 large basil leaves

1/8 tsp. salt

1/8 tsp. pepper

STEPS FOR COOKING

1. Combine turkey, white egg, minced garlic, salt, and pepper until combined.

2. Shape into 2 cutlets. Put cutlets into a skillet; cook 5 minutes per side.

3. Top cutlets with cheese and sliced tomato at the end of cooking.

4. Put 1 cutlet on the bottom of each bun.

5. Top each patty with 2 basil leaves. Cover with bun tops.

DIABETIC DINNER

ORANGE-MARINATED PORK TENDERLOIN

Time required:
45 minutes

Servings: 04

INGREDIENTS

¼ cup freshly squeezed orange juice

2 teaspoons orange zest

2 teaspoons minced garlic

1 teaspoon low-sodium soy sauce

1 teaspoon grated fresh ginger

1 teaspoon honey

1½ pounds pork tenderloin roast

1 tablespoon extra-virgin olive oil

STEPS FOR COOKING

1. Blend together the orange juice, zest, garlic, soy sauce, ginger, and honey.

2. Pour the marinade into a resealable plastic bag and add the pork tenderloin.

3. Remove air as possible as you can and seal the bag. Marinate the pork in the refrigerator, turning the bag a few times, for 2 hours.

4. Preheat the oven to 400°F.

5. Pull out tenderloin from the marinade and discard the marinade.

6. Position big ovenproof skillet over medium-high heat and add the oil.

7. Sear the pork tenderloin on all sides, about 5 minutes in total.

8. Position skillet to the oven and roast for 25 minutes.

9. Put aside for 10 minutes before serving.

COFFEE-AND-HERB-MARINATED STEAK

Time required:
25 minutes

Servings: 03

INGREDIENTS

¼ cup whole coffee beans

2 teaspoons garlic

2 teaspoons rosemary

2 teaspoons thyme

1 teaspoon black pepper

2 tablespoons apple cider vinegar

2 tablespoons extra-virgin olive oil

1-pound flank steak, trimmed of visible fat

STEPS FOR COOKING

1. Place the coffee beans, garlic, rosemary, thyme, and black pepper in a coffee grinder or food processor and pulse until coarsely ground.

2. Transfer the coffee mixture to a resealable plastic bag and add the vinegar and oil. Shake to combine.

3. Add the flank steak and squeeze the excess air out of the bag. Seal it. Marinate the steak in the refrigerator for at least 2 hours, occasionally turning the bag over.

4. Preheat the broiler, then line a baking sheet with aluminum foil.

5. Pull the steak out and discard the marinade.

6. Position steak on the baking sheet and broil until it is done to your liking.

7. Put aside for 10 minutes before cutting it.

8. Serve with your favorite side dish.

GRILLED TUNA KEBABS

Time required:
30 minutes

Servings: 04

INGREDIENTS

2 ½ tablespoons rice vinegar

2 tablespoons fresh grated ginger

2 tablespoons sesame oil

2 tablespoons soy sauce

2 tablespoons fresh chopped cilantro

1 tablespoon minced green chili

1 ½ pound fresh tuna

1 large red pepper

1 large red onion

STEPS FOR COOKING

1. Whisk together the rice vinegar, ginger, sesame oil, soy sauce, cilantro, and chili in a medium bowl – add a few drops of liquid stevia extract to sweeten.

2. Toss in the tuna and chill for 20 minutes, covered.

3. Meanwhile, grease a grill pan with cooking spray and soak wooden skewers in water.

4. Slide the tuna cubes onto the skewers with red pepper and onion.

5. Grill for 4 minutes per side and serve hot.

SHRIMP WITH GREEN BEANS

Time required:
12 minutes

Servings: 04

INGREDIENTS

¾ pound fresh green beans, trimmed

1 pound medium frozen shrimp (peeled and deveined)

2 tablespoons fresh lemon juice

2 tablespoons olive oil

Salt and ground black pepper, as required

STEPS FOR COOKING

1. Arrange a steamer trivet in the Instant Pot and pour a cup of water.

2. Arrange the green beans on top of the trivet in a single layer and top with shrimp.

3. Drizzle with oil and lemon juice.

4. Sprinkle with salt and black pepper.

5. Close the lid and place the pressure valve in the "Seal" position.

6. Press "Steam" and just use the default time of 2 minutes.

7. Press "Cancel" and allow a "Natural" release.

8. Open the lid and serve.

BEEF STEAK FAJITAS

Time required:
25 minutes

Servings: 04

INGREDIENTS

1 lb. lean beef sirloin, sliced thin

1 tbsp. olive oil

1 medium red onion, sliced

1 red pepper, sliced thin

1 green pepper, sliced thin

½ tsp. ground cumin

½ tsp. chili powder

8 (6-inch) whole-wheat tortillas

Fat-free sour cream

STEPS FOR COOKING

1. Preheat a huge cast-iron skillet over medium heat then add the oil.

2. Add the sliced beef and cook in a single layer for 1 minute on each side.

3. Remove the beef to a bowl and cover to keep warm.

4. Reheat the skillet then add the onions and peppers—season with cumin and chili powder.

5. Stir-fry the veggies to your liking then add to the bowl with the beef.

6. Serve hot in small whole-wheat tortillas with sliced avocado and fat-free sour cream.

TILAPIA WITH COCONUT RICE

Time required:
25 minutes

Servings: 04

INGREDIENTS

4 (6 oz.) boneless tilapia fillets

1 tbsp. ground turmeric

1 tbsp. olive oil

2 (8.8 oz.) packets precooked wholegrain rice

1 cup light coconut milk

½ cup fresh chopped cilantro

1 ½ tbsp. fresh lime juice

STEPS FOR COOKING

1. Season the fish with turmeric, salt, and pepper.

2. Cook oil in a large skillet at medium heat and add the fish.

3. Cook for 3 mins per side until golden brown, then remove the fish to a plate and cover to keep warm.

4. Reheat the skillet and add the rice, coconut milk, and a pinch of salt.

5. Simmer on high heat until thickened, about 3 to 4 minutes.

6. Stir in the cilantro and lime juice.

7. Spoon the rice onto plates and serve with the cooked fish.

VEGGIE FAJITAS TACOS

Time required:
25 minutes

Servings: 03

INGREDIENTS	STEPS FOR COOKING

1 onion

Juice of ½ key lime

2 bell peppers

Your choice of approved seasonings (onion powder, cayenne pepper)

6 corn-free tortillas

1 tbsp. grapeseed oil

Avocado

2-3 large portobello mushrooms

1. Remove mushroom stems, spoon gills out if necessary, and clear tops clean. Slice into approximately $1/3$ "thick slices. Slice the onion and bell peppers into thin slices.

2. Pour 1 tbsp. Grapeseed oil into a big-size skillet on medium heat and onions and peppers. Cook for 2 minutes. Mix in seasonings and mushrooms. Stir frequently, and cook for another 7–8 minutes or until tender.

3. Heat the spoon and tortillas the fajita material into the middle of the tortilla. Serve with key lime juice and avocado.

MUFFINS SANDWICH

Time required:
12 minutes

Servings: 01

INGREDIENTS

Nonstick Spray Oil
slice of white
cheddar cheese slice
of Canadian bacon
1 English muffin,
divided
15 ml hot water
large egg
Salt and pepper to
taste

STEPS FOR COOKING

1. Spray the inside of an 85g mold with oil spray and place it in the air fryer.
2. Preheat the air fryer, set it to 160C.
3. Add the Canadian cheese and bacon to the preheated air fryer.
4. Pour the hot water and the egg into the hot pan and season with salt and pepper.
5. Select Bread, set to 10 minutes.
6. Take out the English muffins after 7 minutes, leaving the egg for the full time.
7. Build your sandwich by placing the cooked egg on top of the English muffins and serve

ROASTED PORTOBELLO SALAD

Time required:
10 minutes

Servings: 04

INGREDIENTS

11/2lb. Portobello
mushrooms stem
trimmed

3 heads Belgian
endive, sliced

small red onion,
sliced

4 oz. blue cheese

8 oz. mixed salad
greens

Dressing:

3 tbsp. red wine
vinegar tbsp.
Dijon mustard

2/3 cup olive oil

Salt and pepper to
taste

STEPS FOR COOKING

1. Preheat the oven to 450F.

2. Prepare the dressing by whisking together vinegar, mustard, salt, and pepper.

3. Slowly add olive oil while whisking.

4. Cut the mushrooms and arrange them on a baking sheet, stem-side up. Coat the mushrooms with some dressing and bake for 15 minutes.

5. In a salad bowl toss the salad greens with onion, endive, and cheese. Sprinkle with the dressing.

6. Add mushrooms to the salad bowl.

GROUND TURKEY SALAD

Time required:
45 minutes

Servings: 06

INGREDIENTS

lb. lean ground turkey

1/2 inch ginger, minced

2 garlic cloves, minced onion, chopped

tbsp. olive oil

bag lettuce leaves (for serving)

¼ cup fresh cilantro chopped

2 tsp. coriander powder

1 tsp. red chili powder

1 tsp. turmeric powder

Salt to taste

4 cups water

STEPS FOR COOKING

1. In a skillet sauté the garlic and ginger in olive oil for 1 minute. Add onion and season with salt, then cook for 10 minutes over medium heat.

2. Add the ground turkey and sauté for 3 more minutes. Add the spices (turmeric, red chili powder, and coriander powder).

3. Add 4 cups water and cook for 30 minutes, covered.

4. Prepare the dressing by combining yogurt, sour cream, mayo, lemon juice, chili flakes, salt, and pepper.

5. To serve arrange the salad leaves on serving plates and place the cooked ground turkey on them. Top with the dressing.

Dressing:

2 tbsp. fat-free yogurt

1 tbsp. sour cream, non-fat

1 tbsp. low-fat mayonnaise

Lemon juiced

tsp. red chili flakes

Salt and pepper to taste

WHITE BEAN RISOTTO

Time required:
70 minutes

Servings: 04

INGREDIENTS

400 g white beans

5 cloves of garlic

Sea salt, pepper,
cayenne pepper

4 tbsp olive oil

2 tbsp pasture
butter

200 g risotto rice

500 ml of broth

3 onions

5 tomatoes

2 teaspoons of
chopped thyme

50 g grated
parmesan cheese

STEPS FOR COOKING

1. Soak the beans overnight and drain
   them the next day. Peel the garlic cut
   3 cloves in half, mash the others.

2. In a saucepan with plenty of salted
   water, cook the beans and halved
   garlic for about 35-40 minutes over
   medium heat, then drain and drain
   well.

3. Heat 2 tablespoons of oil and 1
   tablespoon of butter in the pot and
   sauté the rice until translucent. Pour
   in about 250 ml of stock, bring to the
   boil and cook over low heat for about
   20 minutes while stirring, then pour in
   the rest of the broth in between. Keep
   the finished risotto warm.

4. In the meantime, peel and cut the
   onions into eighths. Cut the tomatoes
   crosswise at the top, then pour hot

water over them and peel them. Then cut into cubes.

5. Heat the remaining butter and oil in a pan, add the crushed garlic cloves and onions and sauté. Season to taste with the spices. Then add the tomatoes, thyme, and beans and cook for a few minutes.

6. Arrange the risotto and the beans and serve sprinkled with parmesan.

VEGETABLE NOODLE PAN

Time required:
30 minutes

Servings: 04

INGREDIENTS

20 g sesame seeds

200 g soy cream

1 organic lemon

4 tbsp mixed chopped herbs

Sea salt, pepper

400 g egg-free pasta of your choice

2 carrots

2 zucchini

½ l vegetable stock

350 g smoked tofu

2 tbsp rapeseed oil

STEPS FOR COOKING

1. Toast the sesame seeds in a pan. Rinse the lemon with hot water and finely grate the peel, squeeze out the juice.

2. Mix the soy cream with lemon juice, lemon zest, and herbs, then season with salt and pepper.

3. Cook the pasta in plenty of salted water for 8-10 minutes. Peel the carrots and cut them into strips with the zucchini.

4. Bring the stock to the boil and cook the carrots and zucchini in it for about 3-4 minutes.

5. Dice the tofu and fry all over in the pan with the oil. When ready, remove from the pan and set aside. Now sauté the vegetables and pasta in the frying fat. Mix in the tofu, heat, and season with salt and pepper.

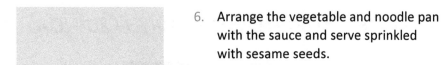

6. Arrange the vegetable and noodle pan with the sauce and serve sprinkled with sesame seeds.

CHICKEN BURRITO BOWL WITH QUINOA

Time required:
25 minutes

Servings: 06

INGREDIENTS

1 tablespoon chipotle chills in adobo

1 tablespoon olive oil

½ teaspoon garlic powder

½ teaspoon ground cumin

1-pound boneless skinless chicken breast

2 cups cooked quinoa

2 cups shredded romaine lettuce

1 cup black beans

1 cup diced avocado

3 tablespoons fat-free sour cream

STEPS FOR COOKING

1. Stir together the chipotle chills, olive oil, garlic powder, and cumin in a small bowl.

2. Preheat a grill pan to medium-high and grease with cooking spray.

3. Season the chicken with salt and pepper and add to the grill pan.

4. Grill for 5 minutes then flip it and brush with the chipotle glaze.

5. Cook for the other 5 minutes until cooked through, then remove to a cutting board and chop the chicken.

6. Assemble the bowls with 1/6 of the quinoa, chicken, lettuce, beans, and avocado.

7. Top each with a half tablespoon of fat-free sour cream to serve.

CHICKEN STEAKS

Time required:
20 minutes

Servings: 03

INGREDIENTS

3 chicken fillets

1 tablespoon BBQ seasonings

1 tablespoon olive oil

1 tablespoon apple cider vinegar

STEPS FOR COOKING

1. Beat the chicken fillets with the kitchen hammer gently.

2. Then rub the fillets with BBQ seasoning and sprinkle with apple cider vinegar.

3. Preheat the grill till 380F.

4. Brush the chicken fillets with olive oil from each side and transfer to the hot grill.

5. Cook the chicken steaks for 4 minutes from each side.

SAUTEED LEMON BEEF

Time required:
45 minutes

Servings: 02

INGREDIENTS

1 oz lemon, sliced

14 oz beef sirloin steak

6 oz fennel, chopped

½ cup of water

1 teaspoon ground coriander

1 teaspoon butter

1 teaspoon salt

¼ cup tomato, crushed

STEPS FOR COOKING

1. Melt the butter in the pan.
2. Meanwhile, chop the beef sirloin steak roughly and add in the butter.
3. Sprinkle it with ground coriander, salt, and add crushed tomatoes. Mix up.
4. Then add water and fennel.
5. After this, add lemon and boil the ingredients for 5 minutes.
6. Transfer the pan in the preheated to 365F oven and cook the meal for 25 minutes.
7. Mix up the beef gently before serving.

CREAM CHEESE PORK TENDERLOIN

Time required:
30 minutes

Servings: 04

INGREDIENTS

7 oz pork tenderloin

1 tablespoon cream cheese

1 teaspoon butter

¼ teaspoon salt

¼ teaspoon ground paprika

¾ teaspoon dried dill

¼ cup of water

STEPS FOR COOKING

1. Preheat the skillet well.

2. Place the pork tenderloin in the hot skillet and roast the meat for 3 minutes from each side over high heat.

3. Then transfer the meat to the saucepan.

4. Add butter, salt, ground paprika, dried dill, and water.

5. Bring the ingredients to boil and add cream cheese.

6. Wait till the cream cheese is melted and close the lid.

7. Cook the meat for 15 minutes over medium heat.

8. Serve the pork tenderloin with the cream cheese dip.

LAMB BARBECUE RIBS WITH CELERY

Time required:
40 minutes

Servings: 04

INGREDIENTS

11 oz lamb ribs, roughly chopped
1 teaspoon ground celery
1 tablespoon Tomato sauce
1 tablespoon paprika
1 teaspoon cayenne pepper
3 tablespoons avocado oil

STEPS FOR COOKING

1. Place the lamb ribs in the tray.
2. Sprinkle them with ground celery, tomato sauce, paprika, cayenne pepper, and avocado oil.
3. Mix up the lamb ribs with the help of the hand palms.
4. Place the ribs in the oven and set grill mode.
5. Cook the lamb ribs for 30 minutes at 360F. Stir the ribs from time to time with the help of the wooden spatula.
6. Then transfer the cooked lamb ribs to the serving bowls. The cooked meal will be light dry.

GARLIC CLAMS

Time required:
15 minutes

Servings: 04

INGREDIENTS

3 lbs. clams, clean
4 garlic cloves
1/4 cup olive oil
1/2 cup fresh lemon juice
1 cup white wine
Pepper Salt

STEPS FOR COOKING

1. Add oil into the inner pot of the instant pot and set the pot on sauté mode.
2. Add garlic and sauté for 1 minute.
3. Add wine and cook for 2 minutes.
4. Add remaining ingredients and stir well.
5. Seal pot with lid and cook on high for 2 minutes.
6. Once done, allow to release pressure naturally. Remove lid.
7. Serve and enjoy.

TEMPEH WITH BELL PEPPERS

Time required:
25 minutes

Servings: 03

INGREDIENTS

2 tablespoons balsamic vinegar

2 tablespoons low-sodium soy sauce

2 tablespoons tomato sauce

1 teaspoon maple syrup

½ teaspoon garlic powder

1/8 teaspoon red pepper flakes, crushed

1 tablespoon vegetable oil

8 ounces tempeh, cut into cubes

1 medium onion, chopped

2 green bell peppers, seeded and chopped

STEPS FOR COOKING

1. In a small bowl, add the vinegar, soy sauce, tomato sauce, maple syrup, garlic powder, and red pepper flakes and beat until well combined. Set aside.

2. Heat 1 tablespoon of oil in a large skillet over medium heat and cook the tempeh for about 2–3 minutes per side.

3. Add the onion and bell peppers and heat for about 2–3 minutes.

4. Stir in the sauce mixture and cook for about 3–5 minutes, stirring frequently.

5. Serve hot.

BEEF WITH MUSHROOMS

Time required:
50 minutes

Servings: 04

INGREDIENTS

300 g beef

150 g mushrooms

1 onion

1 teaspoon olive oil

100 g vegetable broth

1 teaspoon basil

1 teaspoon chili

30 g tomato juice

STEPS FOR COOKING

1. For this recipe, you should take a solid piece of beef. Take the beef and pierce the meat with a knife.

2. Rub it with olive oil, basil, and chili, and lemon juice.

3. Chop the onion and mushrooms and pour it with vegetable broth.

4. Cook the vegetables for 5 minutes.

5. Take a big tray and put the meat in it. Add vegetable broth to the tray too. It will make the meat juicy.

6. Preheat the air fryer oven to 180 C and cook it for 35 minutes.

DIABETIC APPETIZERS

ROASTED ASPARAGUS AND RED PEPPERS

Time required:
20 minutes

Servings: 04

INGREDIENTS

*1 lb. (454g)
asparagus
2 red bell peppers,
seeded
1 small onion
2 tbsp. Italian
dressing*

STEPS FOR COOKING

1. Ready oven to (205ºC). Wrap baking sheet with parchment paper and set aside.

2. Combine the asparagus with the peppers, onion, dressing in a large bowl, and toss well.

3. Arrange the vegetables on the baking sheet and roast for about 15 minutes. Flip the vegetables with a spatula once during cooking.

4. Transfer to a large platter and serve.

SEARED CHICKEN WITH ROASTED VEGETABLES

Time required:
50 minutes

Servings: 01

INGREDIENTS

1 (8-oz) boneless, skinless chicken breasts

¾ lb. small Brussels sprouts

2 large carrots

1 large red bell pepper

1 small red onion

2 garlic cloves halved

2 tbsp. extra virgin olive oil

½ tsp. dried dill

¼ tsp. pepper

¼ tsp. salt

STEPS FOR COOKING

1. Preheat oven to 425°F.

2. Match Brussels sprouts cut in half, red onion cut into wedges, sliced carrots, bell pepper cut into pieces, and halved garlic on a baking sheet.

3. Sprinkle with 1 tbsp. oil and with ⅛ tsp. salt and ⅛ tsp. pepper. Bake until well-roasted, cool slightly.

4. In the Meantime, sprinkle chicken with dill, remaining ⅛ tsp. salt and ⅛ tsp. pepper. Cook until the chicken is done. Put roasted vegetables with drippings over chicken.

PARTY SHRIMP

Time required:
25 minutes

Servings: 03

INGREDIENTS

16 oz. uncooked shrimp, peeled and deveined

1-1/2 teaspoons of juice from a lemon

1/2 teaspoon basil, chopped teaspoon coriander, chopped

1/2 cup tomato tablespoon of olive oil

1/2 teaspoon Italian seasoning

1/2 teaspoon paprika

sliced garlic clove

¼ teaspoon pepper

STEPS FOR COOKING

1. Bring together everything except the shrimp in a dish or bowl.

2. Add the shrimp. Coat well by tossing. Set aside.

3. Drain the shrimp. Discard the marinade.

4. Keep them on a baking sheet. It should not be greased.

5. Broil each side for 4 minutes. The shrimp should become pink.

TURNIPS WITH PEARS ON LETTUCE

Time required:
25 minutes

Servings: 04

INGREDIENTS

600 g turnips

2 carrots

200 ml vegetable stock

2 pears

1 red onion

2 tbsp walnut oil

1 tbsp balsamic vinegar

2 teaspoons of sweet mustard

Sea salt, pepper

1 teaspoon oregano

50 g walnuts

200 g rocket

STEPS FOR COOKING

1. Cut the beets and carrots into long strips with a peeler and then cook them in a saucepan in the vegetable stock.

2. In the meantime, peel and dice the pears, then peel the onion and cut it into rings.

3. Mix walnut oil, balsamic vinegar, and mustard into a vinaigrette and season with oregano, pepper, and salt.

4. Chop the walnuts very finely and roast them in a fat-free pan.

5. Spread the rocket on a large plate. Arrange the beets with the diced carrots and pear, onion rings on the salad, and pour the vinaigrette over it. Now sprinkle with the nuts and serve.

BUTTER-ORANGE YAMS

Time required:
53 minutes

Servings: 08

INGREDIENTS

2 medium jewel yams

2 tablespoons unsalted butter

Juice of 1 large orange

1½ teaspoons ground cinnamon

¼ teaspoon ground ginger

¾ teaspoon ground nutmeg

1/8 teaspoon ground cloves

STEPS FOR COOKING

1. Set oven at 180ºC.
2. Arrange the yam dices on a rimmed baking sheet in a single layer. Set aside.
3. Add the butter, orange juice, cinnamon, ginger, nutmeg, and garlic cloves to a medium saucepan over medium-low heat. Cook for 3 to 5 minutes, stirring continuously.
4. Spoon the sauce over the yams and toss to coat well.
5. Bake in the prepared oven for 40 minutes.
6. Let the yams cool for 8 minutes on the baking sheet before removing and serving.

SIMPLE SAUTÉED GREENS

Time required:
20 minutes

Servings: 04

INGREDIENTS

2 tablespoons extra-virgin olive oil

1 pound (454 g) Swiss chard

1-pound (454 g) kale

½ teaspoon ground cardamom

1 tablespoon lemon juice

STEPS FOR COOKING

1. Heat up olive oil in a big skillet over medium-high heat.

2. Stir in Swiss chard, kale, cardamom, lemon juice to the skillet, and stir to combine. Cook for about 10 minutes, stirring continuously, or until the greens are wilted.

3. Sprinkle with salt and pepper and stir well.

4. Serve the greens on a plate while warm.

PARMESAN TOMATO CHIPS

Time required:
5 hours

Servings: 06

INGREDIENTS

1 ½ pounds
tomatoes, sliced

1/4 cup extra-virgin
olive oil

1 tablespoon Italian
seasoning mix

For Vegan
Parmesan:

1/2 cup pumpkin
seeds

1 tablespoon
nutritional yeast

Salt and black
pepper, to taste

1 teaspoon garlic
powder

STEPS FOR COOKING

1. Drizzle the sliced tomatoes with olive oil.

2. Now, preheat your oven to 200 degrees F. Coat a baking pan with a Silpat mat.

3. Pulse all the parmesan ingredients in your food processor until you reach a Parmesan cheese consistency.

4. Mix the parmesan with the Italian seasoning mix. Then, toss the seasoned tomato slices with the parmesan mixture until they are well coated.

5. Arrange the tomato slices on the baking pan and bake for 5 hours. Store in an airtight container.

TOFU STUFFED ZUCCHINI WITH CASHEW NUTS

Time required:
50 minutes

Servings: 04

INGREDIENTS

1 tablespoon olive oil

2 packages firm tofu, drained and crumbled

2 garlic cloves, pressed

1/2 cup scallions, chopped

2 cups tomato puree

1/4 teaspoon turmeric

1/4 teaspoon chili powder

Sea salt and cayenne pepper, to taste

4 zucchinis, cut into halves lengthwise

STEPS FOR COOKING

1. Heat the oil in a pan that is preheated over moderate heat; now, cook the tofu, garlic, and scallions for 4 to 6 minutes.

2. Stir in 1 cup of the tomato puree and scooped zucchini flesh; add all seasonings and cook an additional 6 minutes, until the tofu is slightly browned.

3. Preheat the oven at 360 degrees F.

4. Divide the tofu mixture among the zucchini shells. Place the stuffed zucchini shells in a baking dish that is previously greased with cooking spray. Pour in the remaining 1 cup of tomato puree.

5. Bake approximately 30 minutes. Sprinkle with the nutritional yeast and

and scoop out the insides

1 tablespoon nutritional yeast

2 ounces cashew nuts, salted and chopped

cashew nuts; bake an additional 5 to 6 minutes. Enjoy!

CHICKEN WITH COCONUT SAUCE

Time required:
35 minutes

Servings: 02

INGREDIENTS

½ lb. chicken breasts

⅓ cup red onion

1 tbsp. paprika
(smoked)

2 tsp. cornstarch

½ cup light coconut
milk

1 tsp. extra virgin
olive oil

2 tbsp. fresh cilantro

1 can tomatoes and
green chilis

¼ cup water

STEPS FOR COOKING

1. Cut chicken into little cubes; sprinkle with 1 ½ tsp. paprika.

2. Heat oil, add chicken and cook for 3 to 5 minutes.

3. Remove from skillet, and fry the finely chopped onion for 5 minutes.

4. Return chicken to pan. Add tomatoes, 1 ½ tsp. paprika, and water. Bring to a boil, and then simmer for 4 minutes.

5. Mix cornstarch and coconut milk; stir into chicken mixture, and cook until it has done.

6. Sprinkle with chopped cilantro.

GARDEN WRAPS

Time required:
30 minutes

Servings: 08

INGREDIENTS

Cucumber, chopped
sweet corn cabbage,
shredded

tablespoon lettuce,
minced

1 tomato, chopped

3 tablespoons of rice
vinegar

2 teaspoons peanut
butter

1/3 cup onion paste

1/3 cup chili sauce

2 teaspoons of low-
sodium soy sauce

STEPS FOR COOKING

1. Cut corn from the cob. Keep in a bowl.
2. Add the tomato, cabbage, cucumber, and onion paste.
3. Now whisk the vinegar, peanut butter, and chili sauce together.
4. Pour this over the vegetable mix. Toss for coating.
5. Let this stand for 10 minutes.
6. Take your slotted spoon and place 1/2 cup salad in every lettuce leaf.
7. Fold the lettuce over your filling.

DIABETIC SIDE DISHES

BROWN RICE AND LENTIL SALAD

Time required:
20 minutes

Servings: 04

INGREDIENTS

cup water

1/2 cup instant brown rice

2 tablespoons olive oil

2 tablespoons red wine vinegar

tablespoon Dijon mustard

1 tablespoon minced onion

1/2 teaspoon paprika

Salt and pepper

(15-ounce) can brown lentils, rinsed and drained

medium carrot, shredded

2 tablespoons fresh chopped parsley

STEPS FOR COOKING

1. Stir together the water and instant brown rice in a medium saucepan.

2. Cover and bring to a boil then simmer for 10 minutes.

3. Remove from heat and set aside while you prepare the salad.

4. Whisk together the olive oil, vinegar, Dijon mustard, onion, paprika, salt, and pepper in a medium bowl.

5. Toss in the cooked rice, lentils, carrots, and parsley.

6. Adjust seasoning to taste then stir well and serve warm.

CURRY ROASTED CAULIFLOWER FLORETS

Time required:
30 minutes

Servings: 06

INGREDIENTS

STEPS FOR COOKING

8 cups cauliflower florets

2 tablespoons olive oil

1 teaspoon curry powder

1/2 teaspoon garlic powder

Salt and pepper

1. Preheat the oven to 425F, then line a baking sheet with foil.

2. Toss the cauliflower with olive oil and spread on the baking sheet.

3. Sprinkle with curry powder, garlic powder, salt, and pepper.

4. Roast for 25 minutes or until just tender. Serve hot.

COFFEE-STEAMED CARROTS

Time required:
13 minutes

Servings: 04

INGREDIENTS

1 cup brewed coffee

1 teaspoon light brown sugar

½ teaspoon kosher salt

Freshly ground black pepper

1-pound baby carrots

Chopped fresh parsley

1 teaspoon grated lemon zest

STEPS FOR COOKING

1. Pour the coffee into the electric pressure cooker. Stir in the brown sugar, salt, and pepper. Add the carrots.

2. Close the pressure cooker. Set to sealing.

3. Cook on high pressure for minutes.

4. Once complete, click Cancel and quickly release the pressure.

5. Once the pin drops, open and remove the lid.

6. Using a slotted spoon, portion carrots to a serving bowl. Topped with the parsley and lemon zest, and serve.

MASHED PUMPKIN

Time required:
25 minutes

Servings: 02

INGREDIENTS

2 cups chopped pumpkin

0.5 cup water

2tbsp powdered sugar-free sweetener of choice

1 tbsp cinnamon

STEPS FOR COOKING

1. Place the pumpkin and water in your Instant Pot.
2. Seal and cook on Stew for 15 minutes.
3. Remove and mash with the sweetener and cinnamon.

ROASTED PARSNIPS

Time required:
38 minutes

Servings: 02

INGREDIENTS

1 lb parsnips

1 cup vegetable stock

2 tbsp herbs

2 tbsp olive oil

STEPS FOR COOKING

1. Put the parsnips in the steamer basket and add the stock into the Instant Pot.

2. Steam the parsnips in your Instant Pot for 15 minutes.

3. Depressurize and pour away the remaining stock.

4. Set to sauté and add the oil, herbs, and parsnips.

5. Cook until golden and crisp.

SPINACH CHIPS WITH GARLIC-AVOCADO DIP

Time required:
20 minutes

Servings: 06

INGREDIENTS

3 ripe avocados, pitted

2 teaspoons lime juice

Salt and black pepper, to taste

2 garlic cloves, finely minced

2 tablespoons extra-virgin olive oil

1/2 teaspoon red pepper flakes

For Spinach Chips:

2 cups baby spinach, washed and dried

1 tablespoon olive oil

Sea salt and garlic powder, to taste

STEPS FOR COOKING

1. Mash the avocado pulp with a fork. Add the fresh lime juice, salt, pepper, garlic, and 2 tablespoons of olive oil.

2. Mix until everything is well incorporated. Transfer to a serving bowl and sprinkle with red pepper flakes.

3. Then, preheat your oven to 300 degrees F. Line a baking sheet with a Silpat mat.

4. Arrange the spinach leaves on the baking sheet; toss with 1 tablespoon of olive oil, salt, and garlic powder.

5. Bake for 8 to 12 minutes so the leaves have dried up. Serve with the well-chilled avocado dip. Bon appétit!

RAINBOW VEGETABLE FRITTERS

Time required:
32 minutes

Servings: 02

INGREDIENTS

1 zucchini, grated, and squeezed

1 cup corn kernels

1/2 cup canned green peas

4 tablespoons all-purpose flour

2 tablespoons fresh shallots, minced

1 teaspoon fresh garlic, minced

1 tablespoon peanut oil

Sea salt

Ground black pepper

1 teaspoon cayenne pepper

STEPS FOR COOKING

1. In a mixing bowl, thoroughly combine all ingredients until everything is well incorporated.

2. Shape the mixture into patties. Spritz the Air Fryer basket with cooking spray.

3. Cook in the preheated Air Fryer at 365 degrees F for 6 minutes. Turn them over, then cook for a further 6 minutes.

4. Serve immediately and enjoy!

SPICY SPINACH

Time required:
30 minutes

Servings: 03

INGREDIENTS

tablespoon olive oil

red onion, chopped finely

6 garlic cloves, minced

(1-inch) piece fresh ginger, minced

1 teaspoon garam masala

1 teaspoon ground coriander

½ teaspoon ground cumin

¼ teaspoon ground turmeric

6 cups fresh spinach, chopped

Salt and ground black pepper, as required

1-2 tablespoons water

STEPS FOR COOKING

1. Heat the olive oil in a large nonstick skillet over medium heat and sauté the onion for about 6-7 minutes.

2. Add the garlic, ginger, and spices and sauté for about 1 minute.

3. Add the spinach, salt, and black pepper, and water and cook, covered for about 10 minutes.

4. Uncover and stir fry for about 2 minutes. Serve hot. Meal Prep Tip:

5. Transfer the spinach mixture into a large bowl and set aside to cool completely. Divide the mixture into 3 containers evenly.

6. Cover the containers and refrigerate for about 1-2 days. Reheat in the microwave before serving.

GINGERED CAULIFLOWER

Time required:
25 minutes

Servings: 02

INGREDIENTS

2 cups cauliflower,
cut into
1-inch florets Salt, as
required
2 tablespoons olive
oil
1 teaspoon fresh
ginger root, sliced
thinly
2 fresh thyme sprigs

STEPS FOR COOKING

1. In a pan of water, add the cauliflower and salt over medium heat and bring to a boil.

2. Cover and cook for about 10-12 minutes.

3. Drain the cauliflower well and transfer it onto a serving platter.

4. Meanwhile, in a small skillet, melt the coconut oil over medium-low heat.

5. Add the ginger and thyme sprigs and swirl the pan occasionally for about 2-3 minutes.

6. Discard the ginger and thyme sprigs.

7. Pour the oil over cauliflower and serve immediately. Meal Prep Tip:

8. Transfer the cauliflower into a large bowl and set aside to cool completely.

9. Divide the cauliflower into 2 containers evenly.

10. Cover the containers and refrigerate for about 1-2 days. Reheat in the microwave before serving.

EGGPLANT CURRY

Time required:
35 minutes

Servings: 02

INGREDIENTS

3 cups chopped eggplant

1 thinly sliced onion

1 cup coconut milk

3 tbsp. curry paste

1 tbsp. oil or ghee

STEPS FOR COOKING

1. Select Instant Pot to sauté and put the onion, oil, and curry paste.

2. Once the onion is soft, stir in the remaining ingredients and seal.

3. Cook on Stew for 20 minutes. Release the pressure naturally.

DIABETIC DESSERT

CHOCOLATE STRAWBERRIES

Time required:
10 minutes

Servings: 04

INGREDIENTS	STEPS FOR COOKING

100 g dark chocolate couverture

300 g fresh strawberries

1. Melt the chocolate slowly in a warm water bath.
2. Wash the strawberries, pat dry and then dip them into the chocolate one by one.
3. Now place the strawberries on baking paper to dry and enjoy afterward.

QUARK BALLS

Time required:
45 minutes

Servings: 24

INGREDIENTS

100 g raisins

800 g boiled jacket potatoes

175 g flour

1 teaspoon Baking powder

500 g low-fat quark

2 eggs

½ teaspoon sea salt

nutmeg

½ organic lemon

1 packet of vanilla sugar

50 g clarified butter

cinnamon

STEPS FOR COOKING

1. Pour hot water over the raisins, then let them soak.

2. In the meantime, peel the potatoes and grate them in a bowl. Rub the flour and baking powder over it. Spread the quark through a sieve.

3. Rinse the lemon with hot water and finely grate the peel. Whisk the eggs and add to the mixture with salt, nutmeg, lemon zest, and vanilla sugar and knead a smooth dough. Dust the raisins with a little flour and knead in.

4. Shape the dough into a roll on a floured surface, then cut the roll into wide slices and press them flat.

5. Heat the clarified butter in a pan and fry the legs until golden brown on both sides. Sprinkle with cinnamon before serving.

COCOA CAKE

Time required:
10 minutes

Servings: 06

INGREDIENTS

3.5 oz. butter

3 eggs

3 oz. sugar

1 tbsp. cocoa powder

3 oz. flour

½ tbsp. lemon juice

STEPS FOR COOKING

1. Mix in 1 tablespoon butter with cocoa powder in a bowl and beat.

2. Mix in the rest of the butter with eggs, flour, sugar, and lemon juice in another bowl, blend properly, and move half into a cake pan

3. Put half of the cocoa blend, spread, add the rest of the butter layer, then crest with remaining cocoa.

4. Put into an air fryer and cook at 360° F for 17 minutes. Allow cooling before slicing.

5. Serve.

GINGER CHEESECAKE

Time required:
35 minutes

Servings: 06

INGREDIENTS

2 tbsp. butter

½ cup ginger cookies

16 oz. cream cheese

2 eggs

½ cup sugar

1 tbsp. rum

½ tbsp. vanilla extract

½ tbsp. nutmeg

STEPS FOR COOKING

1. Spread pan with the butter and sprinkle cookie crumbs on the bottom.

2. Whisk cream cheese with rum, vanilla, nutmeg, and eggs beat properly and sprinkle the cookie crumbs.

3. Put in the air fryer and cook at 340° F for 20 minutes.

4. Allow cheesecake to cool in the fridge for 2 hours before slicing. Serve.

TIRAMISU PUDDING

Time required:
20 minutes

Servings: 01

INGREDIENTS

8 ounces cream
cheese

16 ounces cottage
cheese

4 tablespoons
almond milk

1½ cup Splenda

1 teaspoon instant
coffee

2 tablespoons cocoa
powder

STEPS FOR COOKING

1. In your food processor, mix cottage cheese with cream cheese, cocoa powder, and coffee and blend very well.

2. Add Splenda and almond milk, blend again and divide into dessert cups.

3. Keep in the fridge until you serve.

LEMON SORBET

Time required:
5 minutes

Servings: 04

INGREDIENTS

1 lemon; peeled and roughly chopped

4 cups ice

Stevia to the taste

STEPS FOR COOKING

1. In your blender, mix lemon piece with stevia and ice and blend until everything is combined.
2. Divide into glasses and serve very cold.

SUGAR-FREE CARROT CAKE

Time required:
4 hours

Servings: 08

INGREDIENTS

2 eggs

1/2 almond flour

1/2 cup butter, melted

¼ cup heavy cream teaspoon baking powder

teaspoon vanilla extract or almond extract, optional cup sugar substitute

1 cup carrots, finely shredded

1 teaspoon cinnamon

¼ teaspoon nutmeg

1/8 teaspoon allspice teaspoon ginger

STEPS FOR COOKING

1. Grease a loaf pan well and then set it aside.

2. Using a mixer, combine butter together with eggs, vanilla, sugar substitute, and heavy cream in a mixing bowl, until well blended.

3. Combine almond flour together with baking powder, spices, and baking soda in another bowl until well blended.

4. When done, combine the wet ingredients together with the dry ingredients until well blended, and then stir in carrots. Pour the mixer into the prepared loaf pan, and then place the pan into a slow cooker on a trivet. Add 1 cup water inside.

5. Cook for about 4-5 hours on low. Be aware that the cake will be very moist.

1/2 teaspoon baking soda

For cream cheese frosting:

cup confectioner's sugar substitute

¼ cup butter softened teaspoon almond extract

4 oz. cream cheese softened

6. When the cooking time is over, let the cake cool completely.

7. To prepare the cream cheese frosting: blend the cream cheese together with extract, butter, and powdered sugar substitute until frosting is formed.

8. Top the cake with the frosting.

BLUEBERRY CRISP

Time required:
4 hours

Servings: 10

INGREDIENTS

1/4 cup butter, melted

24 oz. blueberries, frozen

3/4 teaspoon salt

1 1/2 cups rolled oats, coarsely ground

3/4 cup almond flour, blanched

1/4 cup coconut oil, melted

6 tablespoons sweetener

cup pecans or walnuts, coarsely chopped

STEPS FOR COOKING

1. Using a non-stick cooking spray, spray the slow cooker pot well.

2. Into a bowl, add ground oats and chopped nuts along with salt, blanched almond flour, brown sugar, stevia granulated sweetener, and then stir in the coconut/butter mixture. Stir well to combine.

3. When done, spread crisp topping over blueberries. Cook for 3-4 hours, until the mixture, has become bubbling hot and you can smell the blueberries.

4. Serve while still hot with the whipped cream or ice cream if desired. Enjoy!

WATERMELON SHERBET

Time required:
8 minutes

Servings: 04

INGREDIENTS

*6 cups watermelon,
sliced into cubes*

14 oz. almond milk

1 tbsp. honey

¼ cup lime juice

Salt to taste

STEPS FOR COOKING

1. Freeze watermelon for 4 hours.
2. Add frozen watermelon and other ingredients to a blender.
3. Blend until smooth.
4. Transfer to a container with a seal.
5. Seal and freeze for 4 hours.

PEANUT BUTTER CUPS

Time required:
15 minutes

Servings: 04

INGREDIENTS

1 packet plain gelatin

¼ cup sugar substitute

2 cups nonfat cream

½ tsp. vanilla

¼ cup low-fat peanut butter

2 tbsp. unsalted peanuts, chopped

STEPS FOR COOKING

1. Mix gelatin, sugar substitute, and cream in a pan.

2. Let sit for 5 minutes.

3. Place over medium heat and cook until gelatin has been dissolved.

4. Stir in vanilla and peanut butter.

5. Pour into custard cups. Chill for 3 hours.

6. Top with the peanuts and serve.

CHOCO PEPPERMINT CAKE

Time required:
40 minutes

Servings: 04

INGREDIENTS

Cooking spray

⅓ cup oil

15 oz. package
chocolate cake mix

3 eggs, beaten

1 cup water

¼ teaspoon
peppermint extract

STEPS FOR COOKING

1. Spray slow cooker with oil.

2. Mix all the ingredients in a bowl.

3. Use an electric mixer on a medium
   speed setting to mix ingredients for 2
   minutes.

4. Pour mixture into the slow cooker.

5. Cover the pot, then cook on low for 3
   hours. Let cool before slicing and
   serving.

CARROT COOKIES

Time required:
1 hour

Servings: 12

INGREDIENTS

1 piece of ginger (about 5 g)

200 g carrots

1 apple (about 200 g)

70 g walnuts

40 g pitted dates

3 tbsp coconut oil

90 g of tender oat flakes

150 g whole wheat flour

1 teaspoon Baking powder

1 teaspoon cinnamon

½ teaspoon salt

4 tbsp maple syrup

STEPS FOR COOKING

1. Peel the ginger and grate it very finely. Peel the carrots. Wash and core the apple. Roughly grate the carrots and apple. Chop the dates and walnuts. Melt the coconut oil in a saucepan.

2. In a bowl, mix together the oatmeal, flour, baking powder, cinnamon, and salt. Now add the remaining ingredients and work into a dough.

3. Line a baking sheet with parchment paper. Preheat the oven to 180 ° C. Now shape 12 biscuits out of the dough and place them on the baking sheet. Then bake for about 35-40 minutes.

GRILLED ALMOND PEACHES

Time required:
25 minutes

Servings: 01

INGREDIENTS

4 peaches

80 g wholemeal biscuits

20 g of chopped almonds

1 tbsp amaretto

3 sprigs of fresh mint

100 g strawberries

100 g cream cheese

1 teaspoon lemon juice

1 teaspoon of liquid honey

Vanilla pulp

STEPS FOR COOKING

1. Halve the peaches and remove the stones.

2. Crumble the biscuits in a plastic bag with the pasta roller. Then mix with the almonds and amaretto and spread on the peaches.

3. Cut 8 large squares out of aluminum foil and wrap 1 piece around the peaches.

4. Then grill on the grill for about 10 minutes.

5. Wash the mint and shake dry.

6. Finely puree the strawberries with cream cheese, lemon juice, honey, vanilla, and mint.

7. Remove the peaches from the foil. Divide the strawberry sauce among 4 plates and place the peaches on top.

STRAWBERRY SLICES DESSERT

Time required:
45 minutes

Servings: 16

INGREDIENTS

3 eggs

60 g xylitol

2 packs of vanilla sugar

120 grams of flour

1 teaspoon of tartar baking powder

5 sheets of gelatin

500 g strawberries

500 g yogurt

400 g of cream

STEPS FOR COOKING

1. Separate the eggs. Beat the egg yolks with 4 tablespoons of warm water until frothy and mix with 40g xylitol and vanilla sugar until creamy.

2. Mix the flour with the baking powder and fold it into the egg cream. Beat the egg whites with 20g xylitol until stiff and carefully fold into the cream.

3. Preheat the oven to 180 ° C. Line a baking sheet with parchment paper.

4. Now spread the dough on the baking sheet and bake in the oven for about 15 minutes. Then turn the biscuit out and let it cool down. Then cut in half lengthways.

5. Soak the gelatine according to the instructions on the packet, then puree about 300 g strawberries and mix with the yogurt.

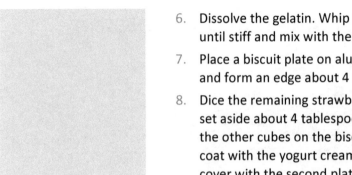

6. Dissolve the gelatin. Whip the cream until stiff and mix with the yogurt.

7. Place a biscuit plate on aluminum foil and form an edge about 4 cm high.

8. Dice the remaining strawberries and set aside about 4 tablespoons. Spread the other cubes on the biscuit and coat with the yogurt cream. Then cover with the second plate. Let the cake cool for about 3-4 hours, then cut into 16 pieces, garnish with the remaining strawberries and serve.

BLUEBERRY SCONES

Time required:
30 minutes

Servings: 10

INGREDIENTS

1 cup white flour

1 cup blueberries

2 eggs

½ cup heavy cream

½ cup butter

5 tbsp. sugar

2 tbsp. vanilla extract

2 tbsp. baking powder

STEPS FOR COOKING

1. Mix in flour, baking powder, salt, and blueberries in a bowl.

2. Mix heavy cream with vanilla extract, sugar, butter, and eggs and turn properly.

3. Blend the 2 mixtures, squeeze till dough is ready, obtain 10 triangles from the mix.

4. Put on baking sheet into the air fryer, and cook them at 320°F for 10 minutes.

5. Serve cold.

MACAROONS

Time required:
10 minutes

Servings: 20

INGREDIENTS

2 tbsp. sugar

4 egg whites

2 cup coconut

*1 tbsp. vanilla
extract*

STEPS FOR COOKING

1. Mix in egg whites with stevia in a bowl and whisk using a mixer.

2. Put the coconut and vanilla extract beat again, get small balls out of the mix, put in the air fryer, and cook at 340°F for 8 minutes.

3. Serve cold.

EASY LEMON CUSTARD

Time required:
40 minutes

Servings: 06

INGREDIENTS

1 ⅓ pint almond milk

5 tablespoons swerve

4 eggs

2 tablespoons lemon juice

4 tablespoons lemon zest

STEPS FOR COOKING

1. In a bowl, mix eggs with milk and swerve and stir very well.

2. Add lemon zest and lemon juice, whisk well, pour into ramekins and place them into a baking dish with some water on the bottom.

3. Bake in the oven at 360 degrees F for 30 minutes

4. Leave the custard to cool down before serving it.

CHOCOLATE GANACHE

Time required:
6 minutes

Servings: 06

INGREDIENTS

4 ounces dark chocolate; unsweetened and chopped

1/2 cup heavy cream

STEPS FOR COOKING

1. Put cream into a pan and heat up over medium heat.
2. Take off heat when it begins to simmer, add chocolate pieces and stir until it melts
3. Serve this very cold as a dessert or use it as a cream for a cake.

GRILLED PEACH AND COCONUT YOGURT BOWLS

Time required:
15 minutes

Servings: 04

INGREDIENTS

2 peaches, halved and pitted

½ cup plain nonfat Greek yogurt

1 teaspoon pure vanilla extract

¼ cup unsweetened dried coconut flakes

2 tablespoons unsalted pistachios, shelled and broken into pieces

STEPS FOR COOKING

1. Preheat the broiler to high. Arrange the rack in the closest position to the broiler.

2. In a shallow pan, arrange the peach halves, cut-side up. Broil for 6 to 8 minutes until browned, tender, and hot.

3. In a small bowl, mix the yogurt and vanilla.

4. Spoon the yogurt into the cavity of each peach half.

5. Sprinkle 1 tablespoon of coconut flakes and 1½ teaspoons of pistachios over each peach half. Serve warm.

CHEESE BERRY FAT BOMB

Time required:
40 minutes

Servings: 12

INGREDIENTS

*1 cup fresh berries,
wash*

1/2 cup coconut oil

*1 1/2 cup cream
cheese, softened*

1 tbsp vanilla

2 tbsp swerve

STEPS FOR COOKING

1. Add all ingredients to the blender and blend until smooth and combined. Spoon mixture into small candy molds and refrigerate until set.

2. Serve and enjoy.